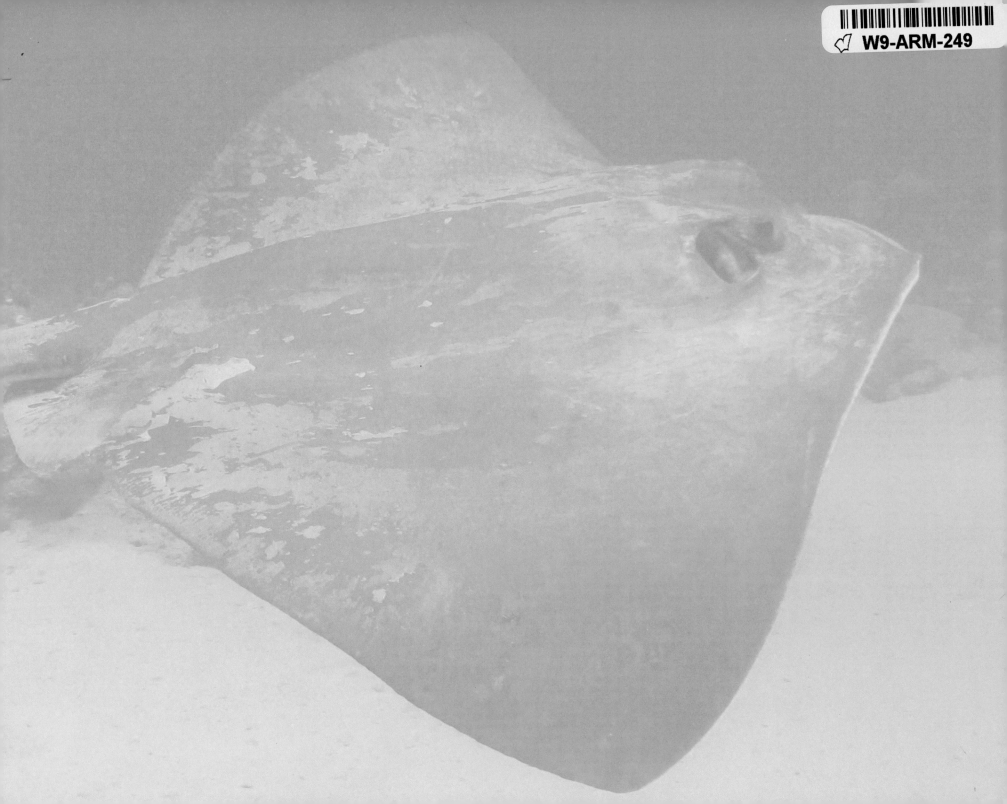

AMAZING UNDERWATER ANIMALS

AMAZING UNDERWATER ANIMALS

Sandy Creek

NEW YORK

An Imprint of Sterling Publishing
387 Park Avenue South
New York, NY 10016

Editorial and design by
Amber Books Ltd
74–77 White Lion Street
London N1 9PF
United Kingdom

Contributing Authors: David Alderton, Susan Barraclough, Per Christiansen, Kieron Connolly,
Paula Hammond, Tom Jackson, Claudia Martin, Carl Mehling, Veronica Ross, Sarah Uttridge
Consulting Editor: Per Christiansen
Series Editor: Sarah Uttridge
Editorial Assistant: Kieron Connolly
Designer: Jerry Williams
Picture Research: Terry Forshaw

ISBN 978-1-4351-4280-0

For information about custom editions, special sales, and premium and corporate purchases, please contact
Sterling Special Sales at 800-805-5489 or specialsales@sterlingpublishing.com.

Manufactured in China

Lot #:
2 4 6 8 10 9 7 5 3 1
09/12

Contents

Introduction

From piranha fish that are just 5–10 in (12–25 cm) long to 10 ft (3 m) long conger eels, all kinds of weird and wonderful creatures inhabit our lakes, swamps, creeks, rivers, seas, and oceans. Crabs, fish, lobsters, eels, starfish, shrimps, and many more, live intriguing lives beneath the surface of the water.

Conger Eel

If you cut the head off the conger eel, it might still bite you. Even when it is dead, the reflexes of this fish are still alert and it can bite. The body of a headless conger eel will keep on wriggling, too. The European conger eel is the largest eel in the world. It is about 10 ft (3 m) long. Eels like to live on rocky inshore beds and in deep caverns.

WHERE DO THEY LIVE?

Eastern Atlantic Ocean from Iceland to West Africa, as well as the Baltic and Mediterranean seas.

Atlantic Ocean

Twisty Killer

▶ After biting into prey, the eel twists its muscular body until it has broken off a chunk of flesh.

Marine Snow

◀ Eel larvae eat marine snow. This is dead or dying animals and plant parts that fall, like snow, deeper into the ocean.

FACTS

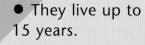

SIZE

- Females are usually twice as long as males.

- They live up to 15 years.

- Conger eels eat fish, squid, octopuses, and crustaceans.

DID YOU KNOW?

Eel larvae look so different from adult eels that scientists used to think they were different types of animals.

They eat hard-shelled animals and crustaceans by smashing the shells open against rocks.

Conger eels sometimes eat other, smaller, conger eels.

Life Stages

▶ Eels begin life as larvae. These have the shape of eels, but most of the body is transparent (see-through). From this stage the larvae will grow into glass eels. The skin of glass eels is still transparent, but the heart and red gills are now visible. They become more colorful at the next stage, when they are called elvers. They finally reach their adult stage, pictured here.

Moray Eel

The moray eel swims by flexing its whole body, like a snake. However, its skin has no scales and is smooth. A slimy coat keeps off germs and parasites. The moray eel has two pairs of nostrils on either side of its snout. It will eat an octopus by biting into it and then looping around the octopus's tentacles. It will then either eat the octopus whole or tentacle by tentacle.

Killer Bite

▶ A moray eel's bite does not just make a wound; it also contains bacteria that can infect and kill divers.

WHERE DO THEY LIVE?

They can be found worldwide in warm, shallow seas.

Eel Colors

◀ There are about 80 species of moray eel. Some of them are dark brown, like the Californian moray. Others have bright patterns.

FACTS

- They can live for up to 25 years.

- They eat fish, octopuses, shrimp, and crabs.

- They are usually 5 ft (1.5 m) long.

SIZE

DID YOU KNOW?

Some moray eels, such as the Tiger moray eel, have horns on their nostrils.

Because it often has its mouth open to breathe, the moray continues its camouflage colors on the inside of its mouth.

To hide from the moray, the parrotfish makes a cocoon out of mucus each night.

Double Jaws

▶ The heads of moray eels are too narrow to swallow in the way other fish do. But they have two jaws, one set further back in their throat. Both jaws have teeth. When feeding, morays launch the jaws in their throat forward into their mouth. These jaws grab the prey and carry it back into the throat and digestive system. Moray eels are the only animal to use their jaws in this way.

Coelacanth

Scientists had thought the coelacanth was extinct. Then, in 1938, a live one was caught off the coast of South Africa. The coelacanth existed before the dinosaurs. It is more than 400 million years old. Its organs are unlike those of any modern animal. Its bone structure is almost the same as it was millions of years ago.

Night Feeder

▶ They feed on deep-sea fish by night. During the day they save energy by hiding away in caves.

DID YOU KNOW?

- They have been seen doing headstands and swimming belly up.

- They are not caught to be eaten because they produce oils that make them taste bad.

- They have been nicknamed "living fossils." For many years, scientists only knew about them from fossils.

WHERE DO THEY LIVE?

They are found along the coastlines of the Indian Ocean and Indonesia.

Indian Ocean

Fat Head

▶ The braincase of the coelacanth is 98.5 percent filled with fat. Only 1.5 percent of it contains brain tissue. Its eyes are very large, helping it see in the dark, deep ocean. Its mouth is very small, but a hinge on the back of its head allows it to open its mouth very wide. Its skin is covered in scales that act like thick armor to protect it.

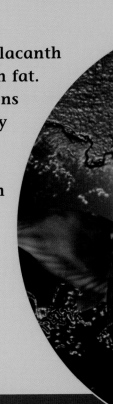

Drifter

◀ It moves like no other fish. Usually it drifts with the up or down movements in the current of the ocean. It has eight fins that help it move in all directions.

FACTS

SIZE

- It grows up to 6 ft (1.8 m) long.

- Its name means "hollow spine."

- Its closest living relative is the lungfish.

Alligator Gar

This is one of the largest freshwater fish in the world. It eats smaller fish, waterbirds, and young alligators. It has been around for 100 million years. Its origins can be traced back to the Cretaceous period. Unlike most fish, it can breathe air and survive above the water for up to two hours.

Scales

▶ Alligator gar scales are shaped like diamonds. Unlike most fish scales, they are interlocking.

WHERE DO THEY LIVE?

It lives in lakes, swamps, and creeks of large rivers, mainly in the lower Mississippi basin.

Gulf of Mexico

Big Fish

◀ They can grow up to 10 ft (3 m) long. An adult weighs about 200 lb (91 kg). They grow quickly and will be 10–12 in (25–30 cm) long after a year. The alligator gar is the largest gar.

FACTS

SIZE

● It lives for more than 50 years.

● Unlike other gars, it has two rows of large teeth in its upper jaw.

● Its eggs are poisonous to humans.

DID YOU KNOW?

It gets its name from its teeth, which are like an alligator's, and its long snout.

Native Americans have used the gar's scales to make jewelry and as arrowheads.

In several southern U.S. states, alligator gar is served in restaurants.

Spear Fish

▶ There are seven living species of gar that live mainly in freshwater in North and Central America and the Caribbean islands. But fossils of ancient gar have been found in Europe and South America, as well as North America. Gar means "spear" in Old English.

Stingray

These animals are called stingrays because of the barbed stings on their tails. These are used for self-defense. The stinger can be 14 in (35 cm) long. Baby stingrays are born with their spines covered up so they don't wound their mother during birth. They have flat bodies that allow them to disturb sand on the seabed. The sand then settles over them, so they are hidden.

Big Ray

▶ The largest species grows up to 15 ft (4.5 m) long, including its tail. The largest wingspan is 7 ft (2 m).

WHERE DO THEY LIVE?

They are found in the shallows of tropical, subtropical, and warm temperate seas.

Finding Prey

◀ Its eyes are on top of its head, but its mouth is on the underside of its body, so it cannot always see its prey. It uses smell and other sensors to find prey.

FACTS

SIZE

● A female will have a litter of between 5 and 13 newborns.

● It is a cartilaginous fish, like a shark. This means it has a skeleton made of cartilage rather than bone.

DID YOU KNOW?

🐚 There are also stingrays that live in freshwater in rivers.

🐚 Although they have a painful sting, stingrays are generally peaceful fish that shy away from aggression.

🐚 Stepping on a stingray can cause a painful sting and cramps from the venom, but it won't usually kill a person.

Eating

▶ It eats mainly mollusks and crustaceans, and sometimes small fish. Some stingray mouths have two powerful, shell-crushing plates. Other stingray species only have sucking mouthparts. When feeding, stingrays settle on the seabed, so that only their eyes and tail are visible. They like to feed on coral reefs.

Barracuda

Barracudas are saltwater fish. They have long bodies and teeth like fangs, similar to piranhas. They are predators and make short, fast dashes to overtake their prey at speeds of up to 27 mph (43 km/h). They prey mainly on fish (some as large as themselves). Adults mainly live alone, but younger fish often meet in groups. They are active at night.

Young Ones

▶ Juvenile (young) barracudas live near the shore (inshore), but adult ones live offshore.

DID YOU KNOW?

It has a swim bladder, which is like a lung. This can be filled with air, which makes the fish float more easily.

Some species live in estuaries. These mix freshwater from rivers and saltwater from the sea, so they are not as salty as the sea.

It is attracted to shiny objects such as jewelry.

WHERE DO THEY LIVE?

They live in tropical and subtropical waters worldwide.

Colors

◄ They are mostly dark blue, dark green, or gray on their upper bodies, with silvery sides and white bellies. The color does vary between species, though.

FACTS

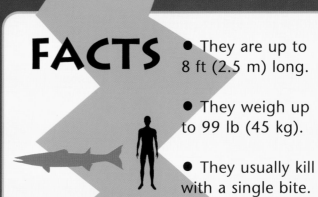

- They are up to 8 ft (2.5 m) long.

- They weigh up to 99 lb (45 kg).

- They usually kill with a single bite.

SIZE

Fish Herders

► Barracudas that have eaten enough of a shoal of small fish sometimes herd the remaining fish into shallow water. They then guard their prey until they are ready to eat again. Barracudas do not usually attack humans. Humans do sometimes eat barracuda, but this is not always safe: toxins build up inside the barracuda from the fish it has eaten.

Grouper

Groupers swallow their prey whole rather than biting off pieces. Their mouth and gills have a powerful system that sucks in their prey from a distance. They do not have many teeth in their jaws, but they have heavy crushing tooth plates in their throats. Groupers eat fish, octopuses, and crustaceans.

WHERE DO THEY LIVE?

In warm shallows all around the world, but mostly in coral reefs.

Gill Muscles

▶ Their gill muscles are so strong that they can almost lock themselves in a cave if they want to.

Patterns

◀ Skin patterns can work as a kind of camouflage because they make the shape of the body harder to recognize. That way, it's more difficult for a predator to spot prey.

FACTS

SIZE

● They can live for 70 years or more.

● They can weigh up to 1,102 lb (500 kg).

● They grow up to 9 ft (2.7 m) long.

DID YOU KNOW?

🐚 They are mostly born female, although some become male when they are adults.

🐚 The grouper is related to the soapfish, which can make a poisonous slime on its skin.

🐚 The biggest grouper is the Queensland. This Australian grouper can weigh 1,102 lb (500 kg).

Eels Inside

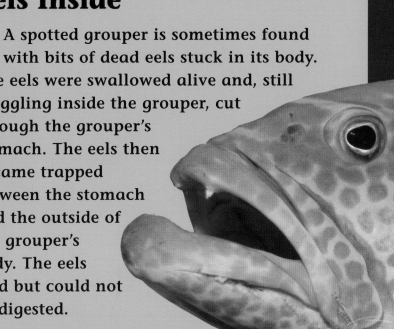

▶ A spotted grouper is sometimes found with bits of dead eels stuck in its body. The eels were swallowed alive and, still wriggling inside the grouper, cut through the grouper's stomach. The eels then became trapped between the stomach and the outside of the grouper's body. The eels died but could not be digested.

Mudskipper

Mudskippers are fish, but they can walk on land and spend as much time out of the water as in it. They can catapult themselves 2 ft (60 cm) into the air. Like amphibians, such as frogs, they can breathe through their skin. They can stay on land for three days. They walk in a hopping, jerky way.

High Eyes

▶ Their eyes are positioned high above the body. This way, the fish can be submerged but the eyes are still above the water.

WHERE DO THEY LIVE?

They live in coastal waters off Africa, India, and Southeast Asia.

Asia

Africa

DID YOU KNOW?

The mudskipper can be recognized by the shape and color of its fins.

It reproduces on land. The male digs a burrow which fills with seawater. The female joins him in the burrow and lays her eggs.

The unusual walk of the mudskipper is known as crutching.

Breathing on Land

▶ Fish don't breathe water the way humans breathe air, but they still need oxygen. They take in water through their mouths and pump it through their gills, where the oxygen is taken out of the water. The mudskipper can survive on land if its gill chamber is full. That way, it can keep using oxygen while out of water. Also, it can absorb oxygen through its skin.

Walking Fins

◀ The mudskipper uses its pectoral fins to walk on land. These fins are linked underneath the fish and this creates a sucker, which helps the fish climb.

FACTS

SIZE

● Mudskippers are a type of goby fish. There are more than 2,000 species of goby.

● Mudskippers keep their body temperature stable on land by digging into the earth.

Swordfish

A swordfish's bill can grow up to 5 ft (1.5 m) long, which is one-third of its total length. Experts are unsure if the bill is a weapon to attack other marine animals or to help the fish swim more smoothly through the water. A young swordfish has teeth, but an adult is toothless. The adult eats its prey whole.

WHERE DO THEY LIVE?

They are found in tropical, subtropical, and temperate oceans all over the world.

Riding Along

▶ Small fish called remoras sometimes attach themselves by suckers to swordfish and hitch a ride.

Ship Ahoy

◀ Swordfish have been known to drive their bills into ships, causing leaks. They probably didn't mean to, but were traveling too fast to stop.

FACTS

SIZE

● They are born with scales but lose these by the time they are adults.

● They are found at depths of up to 1,968 ft (600 m).

● Females are larger than males.

DID YOU KNOW?

They have special organs next to their eyes to heat their eyes and brain.

Predators of swordfish, such as sharks, have been found with the swordfish's bill stuck inside their bodies.

The swordfish pulls its dorsal fin (the fin on its back) close to its body to make it more streamlined.

Longest Bill

▶ A very young swordfish has an upper and lower jaw of the same length. When the swordfish becomes a juvenile (young adult), the upper jaw grows longer than the lower jaw, creating the bill. Like a sword, the bill is smooth, flat, pointed, and sharp. The swordfish has the longest bill in the billfish group, which includes sailfish and marlin.

Lamprey

The lamprey is like a vampire of the sea. It hangs on to other fish with its sucker mouth, then cuts holes in them and drinks their blood. It's a jawless fish but has rows of teeth. The lamprey hunts using its sight and sense of smell. Lamprey fossils have been found from 300 million years ago. They are older than dinosaurs, which arose around 240 million years ago.

Nine Eyes

▶ They were once known as "nine eyes" because of the seven gill holes behind each eye, plus the single nostril between them.

DID YOU KNOW?

- Like sharks, they don't have bones but cartilage.

- Lampreys have been found attached to sharks, but as they cannot cut through shark skin, they were probably just hitching a ride.

- When they reach adulthood, lampreys don't feed but lay eggs and die soon afterward.

WHERE DO THEY LIVE?

They live in the coastal waters of Europe and the American North Atlantic.

North Atlantic Ocean

Sucker Disk

◀ The sucker disk has rows of spiny teeth. These cut away the victim's scales and skin to reach the flesh underneath. Lampreys feed on cod, trout, and salmon.

FACTS

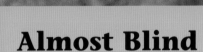

SIZE

- A sea lamprey will drink about 3 lb (1.4 kg) of blood during its adult life.

- A lamprey weighs up to 5 lb (2.5 kg).

- It can grow up to 36 in (90 cm) long.

Almost Blind

▶ For the first seven years of its life, the lamprey is almost blind. It can see only light and dark. The lamprey's eyes develop only when the fish finally turns into an adult. It can create a toxic mucus from its skin to scare off predators. It only lives two years as an adult, before dying.

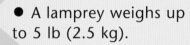

Manta Ray

A gentle giant, the manta ray swims on the surface waters of the warm oceans. Its great wings can launch it high above the waves. The fish lands on the water's surface on its back. This might be to rub lice off the manta's back, but the splash is so big that it can overturn a small boat.

Remora Fish

▶ Remora fish attach themselves to larger rays and eat food that falls from the rays' mouths.

DID YOU KNOW?

The manta ray eats 44–66 lb (20–30 kg) of plankton every day.

It also feeds off the seabed.

It visits cleaning stations, where smaller fish such as wrasse and angelfish swim in the manta's gills and eat off parasites and dead tissue.

WHERE DO THEY LIVE?

It is found mainly offshore in all the warm seas and oceans of the world.

Tiny Teeth

▶ Over thousands of years, the manta ray has changed what it eats. Today, it eats shrimp and tiny plankton. Because of this, its teeth have become smaller. It has rows of tiny teeth almost hidden in its lower jaws. Instead of using these, it filters water into its mouth and out of its gill as it swims. It catches prey on plates in its gills called gill rakers.

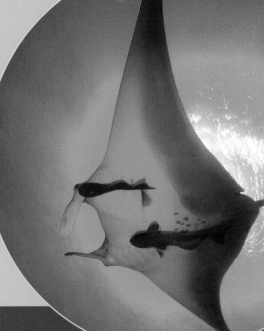

Feeding Frenzy

◀ Where there are a lot of plankton, hundreds of rays will gather in groups. Swimming around together, they create a swirling cyclone and feed.

FACTS

SIZE

- Their disk width can reach 23 ft (7 m).

- They weigh around 2,900 lb (1,300 kg).

- Their predators are larger sharks.

Scorpionfish

The scorpionfish disguises itself as a rock covered in algae. Some can even change their color to blend in with their surroundings. When danger threatens, the spines on the scorpionfish's back stand up. These are only for defense, but they can give a very painful sting. Swelling from a sting can affect a person's entire arm or leg within minutes.

Venom Glands

▶ The venom glands are on spines on its fins. Once used, these glands take six days to recharge.

WHERE DO THEY LIVE?

In shallow bays in temperate to tropical seas, mainly in the Indian and Pacific oceans.

Asia

Pacific Ocean

Indian Ocean

Feeding

◀ It feeds by opening its mouth and then its gills a fraction of a second apart. This creates suction, which pulls its prey into its mouth.

FACTS

SIZE

- It is 4–14 in (10–35 cm) long.

- It weighs on average 3.5 lb (1.5 kg).

- The fin on its back has 11 to 17 spines.

DID YOU KNOW?

- After it has been killed, a scorpionfish's spines are still dangerous for several days.

- Adult lionfish, a type of scorpionfish, will eat smaller lionfish.

- The red scorpionfish regularly sheds its skin like a snake. Sometimes it replaces its skin twice a month as it grows.

In Disguise

▶ The head has fleshy flaps. These provide extra camouflage, helping it look like a rock but also drawing attention away from the scorpionfish's mouth. One species, the decoy scorpionfish, has a dorsal (back) fin that looks like a separate fish altogether. Some species sway their bodies from side to side to look like a piece of debris.

Ocean Sunfish

The ocean sunfish is the heaviest bony fish in the world. It weighs around 2,200 lb (1,000 kg), and is about 6 ft (1.8 m) long. It can change its skin color, especially when it is under attack. This fish does not have scales, but its skin is covered by a layer of slimy mucus.

DID YOU KNOW?

All sunfish can breach. This means they can jump out of the water. They might do this to rid themselves of parasites on their skin.

All sunfish also allow cleaner wrasse fish to eat the parasites found on their skin.

The ocean sunfish's top to bottom fin length is 8 ft (2.5 m).

WHERE DO THEY LIVE?

They live in temperate and tropical waters in every ocean.

Bird Food

▶ By basking on its side on the surface, the sunfish allows sea birds to feed on parasites on its skin.

Sunfish Diet

▶ It mainly eats jellyfish, as well as squid, crustaceans, fish larvae, eel grass, smaller fish, and small invertebrates. The sunfish feeds at many different levels, from the surface of the water to the seabed. However, this diet is poor, so the sunfish has to eat large amounts of food to get enough goodness from it. Its teeth look a bit like a beak. It also has teeth in its throat to help grind up food.

Peaceful Giant

◀ Despite its size, the sunfish is a peaceful animal and not a threat to divers. However, because it's so big it can be a problem if it hits a boat.

FACTS

● Sunfish can live for up to ten years in captivity. We are not sure how long they can live in the wild.

● They can swim up to 2 mph (3.2 km/h).

SIZE

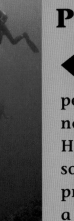

Porcupine-fish

The porcupinefish can swallow water or air to inflate its body. This can almost double its size from top to bottom, which means that fewer predators can get their mouths around it. Also, when it is inflated, the porcupinefish's spines stick out.

Self-defense

▶ Its fins are too small for fast swimming. As it cannot escape quickly, the fish needs to be able to defend itself.

WHERE DO THEY LIVE?

They are found in warm seas across the world, especially on coral reefs.

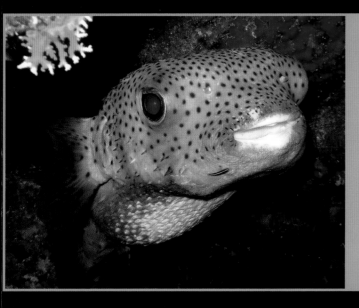

Spineless?

◀ Usually, the porcupinefish looks quite harmless, and so other marine animals, such as dolphins, try to attack it. But it can quickly shoot up its spines.

FACTS

- They are usually 12 in (30 cm) long.

- They live alone and are active at night.

- They eat coral, marine worms, and shellfish.

SIZE

DID YOU KNOW?

🦐 They are also called balloonfish, globefish, and blowfish.

🦐 When they eat coral, the crushed remains often stay in their bodies. One porcupinefish was found with 18 oz (500 g) of coral rock in its stomach.

🦐 Young porcupinefish are sometimes eaten by tuna and dolphins.

Poison

▶ In addition to being able to change their size and stick out their spines, some species of porcupinefish are also poisonous. They have a toxin in their livers that is very strong. Because of this, the porcupinefish has very few predators, although adults are sometimes preyed upon by sharks and orcas (killer whales).

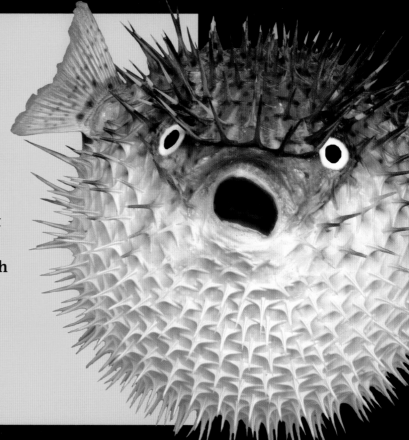

Electric Ray

The electric ray has cells on either side of its head that can produce electric pulses. These can scare off predators. Their electric discharge ranges from 8 to 220 volts, which is twice the voltage in an electric wall socket. In ancient Rome, the electricity produced by the electric ray was used to treat people with foot problems.

Swimming

▶ It is not a strong or fast swimmer. It propels itself by the large fins along its body.

WHERE DO THEY LIVE?

They are found in tropical to temperate seas in both shallow and deep water.

Feeding

◀ They eat small fish and invertebrates, such as snails, worms, and crabs. They often hide their flat bodies beneath the sand, before stunning their prey with electricity.

FACTS

SIZE

● They are up to 6 ft (1.8 m) long.

● There are 69 species of electric ray.

● They weigh up to 198 lb (90 kg).

DID YOU KNOW?

Its eyes are very small, so the ray probably uses chemical sensors to find prey.

Its very big fins flatten out into a disk so that it can bury itself in the sand.

It is also known as the torpedo fish. The torpedo missile gets its name from this.

Electric Shocks

▶ Other rays, skates, and marine animals such as dolphins are also electro-sensitive, but electric rays are the most sensitive. Inside the body is a kind of electric battery. When it sends an electric shock, all the muscles in its body are affected, so it too feels part of the shock. On dry land it can still give a shock if water is poured on it.

Sturgeon

There are 26 different species of sturgeon. Some are 3 ft (1 m) long; others are more than 16 ft (5 m) long. The food caviar is made from the eggs of sturgeon. A female sturgeon may lay as many as a million eggs during her spring spawning. We can see from fossils that sturgeon have changed very little in 200 million years—since the time of the dinosaurs.

Scutes

▶ All sturgeon have rows of hard plates, called scutes, along their sides. They vary in size depending on species.

WHERE DO THEY LIVE?

Sturgeon live in cool northern seas, rivers, and lakes in Europe and North America.

North America

Europe

Wedge Snout

◀ With its snout shaped like a wedge, it stirs up the riverbed. The mouth is under the fish, because it eats off the riverbed. The mouth can be pushed out to suck up prey.

FACTS

SIZE

● Most species are at risk of extinction.

● These fish do not have scales.

● Smoked sturgeon is a delicacy in many areas.

DID YOU KNOW?

🐴 They live for more than 100 years. They are probably the longest-living fish.

🐴 They do not have bones but a frame made of cartilage, like sharks.

🐴 They produce a substance called isinglass, which is used to remove the cloudiness from wine.

Mouthparts

▶ The sturgeon has four barbels (these look like whiskers) that dangle from its snout. The barbels are used to find shells, worms, crustaceans, and small fish. The sturgeon does not have any teeth and so cannot grab hold of its prey. However, large sturgeon can swallow large prey, such as salmon, in one piece.

Piranha

Piranhas are most easily recognized by their sharp teeth. They have a single row of triangular-shaped teeth in each jaw. The upper and lower teeth interlock when the jaws are closed. They are known for their meat-eating, but they are actually omnivores—this means they eat both animals and plants.

WHERE DO THEY LIVE?

Piranhas are found in the rivers of tropical South America.

South America

Tree Hunters

▶ Schools of piranhas hide under riverside trees where birds are nesting. There they can eat any young birds that fall into the water.

Scaly Body

◀ It is a scaly fish and can be 5–10 in (12–25 cm) long. It blends in well with its surroundings. It has a very powerful tail, making it a fast swimmer.

FACTS

SIZE

- They can live up to 12 years in the wild.
- They prefer to live in fast-moving water.
- Their predators are river otters, dolphins, caimans, and cormorants.

DID YOU KNOW?

- In South America, piranhas are a popular food to eat.
- They only occasionally attack humans, and they only do this when they are starving. They are more likely to attack each other.
- They are a nuisance to fishermen because they steal bait and damage fishing nets.

Group Attacks

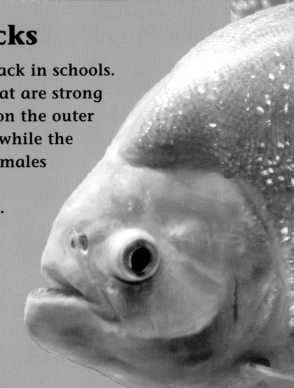

▶ They usually attack in schools. The older fish that are strong and dominant stay on the outer edges of the school, while the younger ones and females are protected in the middle of the school. They eat insects, invertebrates, small animals, and carrion—dead animals that they find in the water.

Tigerfish

The tigerfish gets its name from the stripes on its body. This fish hunts in groups called shoals. By hunting in shoals, the tigerfish can attack prey much larger than itself. It has sharp, interlocking teeth. It eats other fish and some land animals, such as monkeys, that enter the water.

Hearing Aid

▶ It has an air-filled sac in its body that is used for hearing. It listens in case animals that it can eat fall into the water.

WHERE DO THEY LIVE?

Africa

They live in rivers and lakes in western, central, and southern Africa, and in the River Nile.

DID YOU KNOW?

- Although the tigerfish has similar teeth and behavior to the piranha, it is from a different zoological family.

- It was given its Latin name, *Hydrocynus*, which means "water dog," because it hunts in packs like dogs.

- It has occasionally been known to attack humans

Habitat

◀ Building dams and changing the courses of rivers have damaged the tigerfish's habitat. There is now less vegetation and the fish cannot reproduce as easily.

FACTS

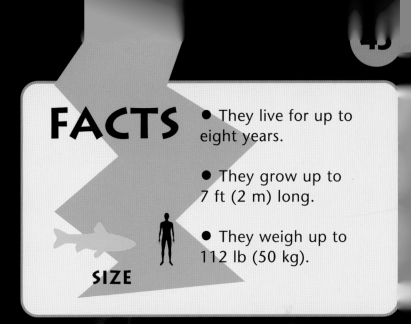

- They live for up to eight years.

- They grow up to 7 ft (2 m) long.

- They weigh up to 112 lb (50 kg).

SIZE

Long Teeth

▶ Its large, long teeth can always be seen, even when its mouth is closed. Young tigerfish move in large numbers and will often attack any animal that enters the water. Adults travel in smaller groups of up to five. Both groups are very dangerous. When a victim is bitten, its blood excites the tigerfish, who feed wildly on the wounded animal.

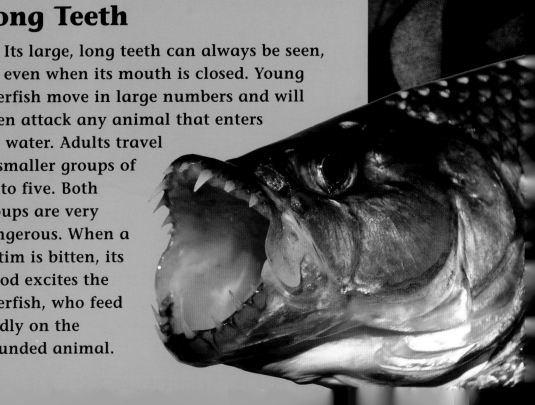

Northern Pike

Northern pike are found in slow-moving streams and lakes. They will lie very still for hours, waiting for prey. They then accelerate very quickly. They eat other fish (including other pike), as well as frogs, water voles, ducklings, and some carrion (animals that are dead when found).

WHERE DO THEY LIVE?

It lives in northern Europe and Asia, and the north of the United States.

USA

Europe

Asia

Choker

▶ Young northern pike have been found dead from choking while trying to eat another pike of the same size.

Predator

◀ It hunts alone. It catches its prey from the side. Its sharp, backward-pointing teeth stop the prey. Then it turns the prey headfirst and swallows it.

FACTS

- They grow to 59 in (150 cm) long.

- They can weigh 55 lb (25 kg).

- Females are two to three times heavier than males.

SIZE

DID YOU KNOW?

- It usually lives from 5 to 15 years, but specimens as old as 30 years have been found.

- It also lives in the Baltic Sea, which has lower salt levels than other seas.

- It gets its name because it looks like the weapon called a pike—a long pole with a sharp head.

Pike Body

▶ The younger pike has yellow stripes on a green body, but the stripes later divide into light spots. It has sensory pores on its head and the underside of the lower jaw. These help it recognize movement in the water. The mouth can be extended, allowing it to capture large prey.

Electric Eel

Batteries have a positive (+) and negative (–) charge and so does the electric eel. Half of its body weight is made up of the organs that produce electricity. It is a fish that can generate up to 600 volts, almost six times more than comes out of a household wall socket. The electric eel usually eats invertebrates, fish, and frogs, but can also eat small mammals.

Sensors

▶ Holes along its back act as sensors. These can tell when other animals move in the water or where obstacles are.

DID YOU KNOW?

Males are much smaller than female electric eels.

Although they have gills, they rise to the water's surface about every 10 minutes to take in air.

Despite having a big mouth, its teeth are very basic and it cannot chew. It just swallows its prey whole.

WHERE DO THEY LIVE?

They are found in the muddy backwaters of the Orinoco and Amazon rivers in South America.

South America

Appearance

◀ It is not a true
eel and is more
closely related to the
catfish. It does not
have any scales. It has
a huge mouth. Males
have a darker color
on the belly.

FACTS

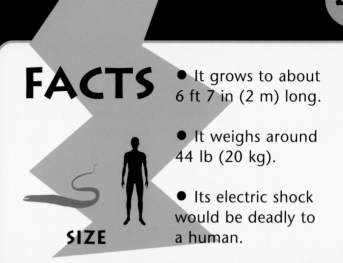

SIZE

• It grows to about
6 ft 7 in (2 m) long.

• It weighs around
44 lb (20 kg).

• Its electric shock
would be deadly to
a human.

Electric Shocks

▶ It can vary the intensity of its
electric shocks. Weaker shocks
are used for hunting and stronger
ones for stunning or defense. Each
shock is a series of short, strong
pulses lasting less than .002 of
a second. The electric
eel can produce
shocks for at
least an hour
before it begins
to tire.

Lungfish

Most fish breathe through their gills, but almost all lungfish breathe through their mouths. They take in air not water, and they have lungs. During dry seasons, African and South American lungfish burrow into mud and go into a kind of sleep where the body uses very little energy. They survive like this until the next rainy season.

Eating

▶ Lungfish are omnivorous. They eat fish, insects, crustaceans, worms, mollusks, amphibians, and plant matter.

WHERE DO THEY LIVE?

They are freshwater fish found in Africa, South America, and Australia.

South America   Africa   Australia

DID YOU KNOW?

೯ In the African lungfish, the upper jaw has two rounded teeth at the front. The lower jaw has many crushing teeth.

೯ All lungfish have lungs similar to those found in some amphibians.

೯ Fossils show that in the Mesozoic period (250–65 million years ago) lungfish lived all around the world.

Breathing

▶ All lungfish have nostrils inside their bodies and most have two lungs. Lungs carry oxygen into the bloodstream and transfer carbon dioxide from the bloodstream back into the atmosphere. They are essential for breathing. The Australian lungfish has only one lung, but it can also breathe through its gills, like other fish.

Eggs

◀ They build a nest for their eggs. The nest is protected by the male until the eggs have hatched. The young fish have gills that disappear as the fish grow.

FACTS

● They can live to more than 70 years old.

● The African lungfish reaches 6 ft (2 m) long.

● Lungfish weigh up to 88 lb (40 kg).

SIZE

Elephantnose Fish

The long "nose" of the elephantnose fish is in fact a jaw that curves down from its tiny mouth. The jaw is very sensitive to chemicals and touch, which helps it to find prey. In its skull and inner ear the elephantnose fish has sensors to recognize the movement of other marine animals.

Sound

▶ For a fish it has good hearing (in the range of 100–2,500 hertz), but humans can hear far better (in the range of 20–20,000 hertz).

WHERE DO THEY LIVE?

It is found in muddy, slow-moving rivers in Central and West Africa.

Africa

Electric Tail

◄ The electric organ in the tail produces only a few microvolts of electricity. This is not enough to shock and stun prey.

FACTS

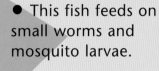
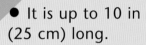

SIZE

● This fish feeds on small worms and mosquito larvae.

● It is up to 10 in (25 cm) long.

● It will live in the same region for many years.

DID YOU KNOW?

The elephantnose fish usually lives for about six to ten years.

It has good eyesight but because it lives in muddy waters it can't rely on its vision to guide it or to see prey or predators.

It is a nocturnal fish, which means that it is active at night.

Electric Signals

▶ The elephantnose fish can sense electric signals in the water. It can even tell male and female elephantnose fish apart from their different electric signals. The electric field that a fish generates also marks its territory as each fish has its own signal.

Stargazer

Stargazers are so called because their eyes are on top of their heads. They bury themselves in the sand with their upward-facing mouth. Then, when prey passes overhead, they jump upward and ambush it. They eat invertebrates and other fish. They are venomous, take in water through nostrils rather than through their mouths, and can produce electrical charges.

Nostrils

▶ Fleshy fringes similar to a comb prevent grains of sand from entering the stargazer's nostrils.

WHERE DO THEY LIVE?

They are found in tropical and temperate waters around the world.

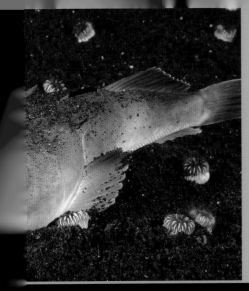

Seabed

◀ The stargazer lies silent, still, and covered in sand and mud. Some have a wormlike spike on the bottom of their mouths. They wiggle this to attract prey.

FACTS

- They are up to 28 in (70 cm) long.

- They weigh up to 20 lb (9 kg).

- If disturbed by divers, they may bite.

SIZE

DID YOU KNOW?

They have venomous spines above some of their fins.

There are 51 species of stargazer.

All animal muscles produce tiny charges of electricity, but only a few creatures, such as the stargazer, can use this energy.

Eyes and Gills

▶ Behind the eyes is a special pouch where the electric organs grow. The stargazer can produce a charge of 50 volts. It has narrow gills that extend backward to form baggy tubes. It takes in water through the mouth and releases it through these gills. But this does not disturb the sand and so the fish's position is not revealed.

Striped Eel Catfish

Young striped catfish do not just swim in shoals. They swim so close together that to a predator they might look like one large animal—one too big to attack. If danger does threaten, each catfish twists and turns, making it hard for the enemy to pick out an individual to attack.

Venom

▶ The brightly colored bars on a young catfish warn enemies that this fish carries venomous spines.

WHERE DO THEY LIVE?

They live in estuaries and warm coastal waters around coral reefs in the Indian and Pacific oceans.

Pacific Ocean

Indian Ocean

Camouflage

◀ The stripes on the young catfish are like the stripes on a zebra. It's difficult to see clearly just one animal in a group because the stripes confuse the viewer.

FACTS

SIZE

- It grows to up to 12 in (30 cm) long.
- It can weigh up to 2 lb (1 kg).
- It eats small fish, shrimp, and worms.

DID YOU KNOW?

• Although it is a saltwater fish, catfish can also survive in freshwater and will swim up rivers.

• The male digs a pit in the seabed for the female to lay eggs in. The male protects the eggs until they hatch.

• Striped eel catfish can release a chemical to let other fish know when there is danger.

Toxic Body

▶ Its wide mouth is full of bristly, tiny teeth. These grasp and crush shrimp and other small prey. Around the mouth hang four pairs of barbels. These have sensors on them. The scaleless skin and the spines on the dorsal (back) fin are covered in a toxic mucus that can be poisonous to humans.

Wels Catfish

Unlike most fish, the wels catfish doesn't have scales. It has a long, slimy, green-brown body and its wide mouth contains hundreds of tiny teeth. The catfish gets its name from its barbels (the whiskers near its mouth) and because it makes almost a purring sound when caught.

Barbels

▶ The barbels around its mouth contain sensors, helping with taste and also navigation.

WHERE DO THEY LIVE?

They are found in freshwater in central and eastern Europe.

Europe

Size

◀ The wels catfish is one of the largest freshwater fish. It grows so big by eating fish, frogs, rats, mice, and ducks. It only has small teeth, so it swallows its prey in one piece.

FACTS

- They grow up to 16 ft (5 m) long.
- They weigh up to 118 lb (300 kg).
- They live for up to 30 years.

SIZE

DID YOU KNOW?

🌊 It generally spends its life alone.

🌊 With its pectoral fins (those on its side) it creates a mini whirlpool that confuses its prey. In the confusion, its massive jaw opens and it swallows its prey.

🌊 The wels catfish has also been introduced into western Europe.

Reproduction

▶ The male makes a nest for the female's eggs by digging out an area at the bottom of a river or lake and filling it with waterweed. After the female lays her eggs, the male guards them until they hatch. The female lays up to half a million eggs at a time. Few of them survive to adulthood. Some are even eaten by older wels.

Sawfish

What looks like a chainsaw on the sawfish is its rostrum. This is covered with pores that allow it to sense the movement of prey hiding on the ocean floor. Then it can use the saw to dig up crustaceans. It usually moves slowly, but it can slash prey with its rostrum. It also defends itself with its rostrum against divers and sharks.

Offspring

▶ Females give birth to live pups. At birth, the rostrum is covered to prevent the pup from injuring its mother.

DID YOU KNOW?

- Sawfish reach adulthood at the age of ten.

- All sawfish species are critically endangered. Capturing sawfish is illegal in the USA and in Canada.

- Sawfish use their large liver filled with oil to control how they float.

WHERE DO THEY LIVE?

They are found in most subtropical and tropical coastal waters; they also swim up rivers.

Feeding

▶ What look like teeth on the rostrum are in fact denticles. Like rays, the sawfish's mouth and nostrils are on their flat undersides. The mouth has small teeth for eating small fish, crabs, worms, and mollusks. Sometimes the sawfish swallows its prey whole. It will sleep during the day and hunt at night. Its intestines are shaped like a corkscrew.

Breathing

◀ The sawfish breathes through two holes behind the eyes called spiracles. These draw the water into the gills. The eyes themselves are undeveloped.

FACTS

- The rostrum is more than 3ft 3in (1m) long.

- It has more than 100 teeth in each jaw.

- There are 20–30 denticles on the rostrum.

SIZE

Harlequin Shrimp

The harlequin shrimp gets its name from its bright colors and pattern, which looks like the costume of a harlequin clown. The colors can act as camouflage among some coral. But it's also possible that they might trick fish into thinking that the shrimp tastes nasty.

WHERE DO THEY LIVE?

It is found on coral reefs and rocky coasts in the Indian Ocean and the western Pacific Ocean.

Pacific Ocean

Indian Ocean

Starfish Meal

▶ A starfish has a thick topside, but the harlequin shrimp turns it upside down and eats from its soft underside.

Pincers

◀ Between its large claws are two pincers. They are short but sharp and strong and can snip off pieces of starfish. They pass the pieces to the mouth to eat.

FACTS

SIZE

- It can grow up to 2.5 in (6 cm) long.
- It lives among rocks down to 30 ft (10 m).
- It only eats starfish.

DID YOU KNOW?

🦐 It has to shed its hard exoskeleton (its shell) to grow. It does this at new moon, when there is no moonlight to help predators see it when it is unprotected.

🦐 To break free from its old exoskeleton it sucks in water to its hindgut, causing the abdomen to expand and the old shell to crack.

Colorful Body

▶ The harlequin shrimp has an eye-catching body. However, not all of it is very useful. The eyes appear at the end of stalks, but they don't work well. The claws are massive but they are probably more for showing off than actually scaring away other animals or for catching them. It relies on its antennae for hearing.

Slipper Lobster

The slipper lobster is recognized by its antennae, which stick forward from the head like wide plates. They are used for shoveling. It also has two smaller antennae for sensing movement. It doesn't have any pincers. To defend itself it uses its hard shell and hides itself on the seabed.

Break a Leg

▶ If a predator twists a lobster's leg, it snaps off at a special point. The lobster can escape and grow another leg.

WHERE DO THEY LIVE?

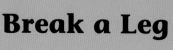

It lives in warm coastal waters worldwide at depths of 16–1,968 ft (5–600 m).

Hitching

◀ Some slipper lobster larvae hitch a lift on the umbrellas of passing jellyfish. They hold on with the tiny hooks on the tips of their legs.

FACTS

- They grow to 6–20 in (15–50 cm) long.

- They can weigh up to 4–5 lb (2 kg).

- There are about 70 different kinds of slipper lobster.

SIZE

DID YOU KNOW?

A slipper lobster's fertilized eggs look like clusters of berries. A female carrying eggs on her legs is known as a "berried" female.

It is active at night and will eat algae, sea plants, some mollusks, and other crustaceans.

It is eaten by bony fish and by humans.

Shell

▶ It may allow barnacles, sand, and weeds to settle on its shell, which add to its camouflage. Its flattened shape helps it to cling to rock walls and to slip into cracks. Like most crustaceans, it sheds its skin as it grows. Then it takes in water to enlarge its body. When its new shell hardens, it spits the water out, leaving space to grow into the new shell.

Spiny Lobster

Like slipper lobsters, spiny lobsters are not true lobsters. They don't have claws on the first four pairs of walking legs and they have larger antennae. Spiny lobsters are also known as rock lobsters or langouste. At night, they crawl along the ocean floor, looking for prey.

WHERE DO THEY LIVE?

They are found in warm to tropical coastal waters of the Pacific, Atlantic, and Indian oceans.

Atlantic Ocean

Pacific Ocean

Indian Ocean

DID YOU KNOW?

- It uses its flattened tail to propel itself backward.

- It has three sets of mouthparts—each a different size—plus a pair of crunching jaws.

- Sometimes it moves into deep water. It has been seen at depths of more than 330 ft (100 m).

Cannibal

▶ It eats any slow-moving, dead or dying creature, including other spiny lobsters.

Antennae

▶ At the base of each antenna, it has a flap that it can rub back and forth on a smooth ridge to make a rasping sound. It makes this sound to scare away predators when it feels threatened. Members of a line of lobsters may also use this to communicate with each other.

Migration

◀ Spiny lobsters migrate in columns of up to 60. The lobsters can travel up to 63 miles (100 km) in a week, covering about 9 miles (15 km) a day.

FACTS

SIZE

● Its body can be up to 20 in (50 cm) long.

● Its antennae can be up to 24 in (60 cm) long.

● It can weigh up to 17 lb (8 kg).

Hermit Crab

A hermit crab makes its home in an empty shell. The weight of the shell keeps the crab on the seabed. When it grows too big for its shell, it finds a larger shell to live in. Its tail naturally curves to the right because there are more shells that twist that way for it to fit in.

Sea Snails

▶ It often lives in sea snail shells. Where there are no big sea snails, the hermit crab will die while looking for a larger home.

WHERE DO THEY LIVE?

It lives in all the seas and oceans of the world from the seashore to the deep sea.

Larvae

◀ A female carries her eggs inside her shell until they hatch into tiny larvae. These drift in the ocean until they are ready to find small shells of their own.

FACTS

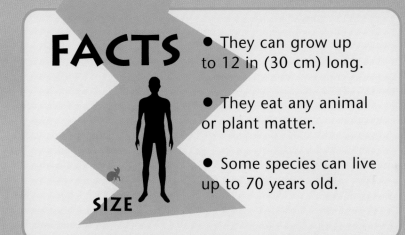

SIZE

- They can grow up to 12 in (30 cm) long.
- They eat any animal or plant matter.
- Some species can live up to 70 years old.

DID YOU KNOW?

- The hermit crab lives in shells because it has to protect its soft abdomen.

- When the largest crab moves into a new shell, the second-largest crab moves into the newly available shell, and each smaller crab moves up into the next best shell.

- Some species live in sponges, not shells.

Hermit Crab Body

▶ It has compound eyes like those of an insect. They are on the ends of stalks to offer all-around vision. The long antennae are used to investigate food and possible new homes. The pincers tear food apart and are also used as weapons. One pincer is usually larger than the other and acts as a door when the crab hides in its shell.

Cone Shell

The cone shell is a venomous sea snail. It is capable of stinging—some even killing—humans. It uses a radula (a grating tongue) and a venom gland to attack and paralyze prey. Sometimes the radula fires out like a harpoon. Then it surrounds its prey and it is pulled in one piece into the cone shell. A fish will take several days to digest.

Shell Layers

▶ The shell builds up layers for protection. However, a large fish can crunch it open.

WHERE DO THEY LIVE?

Most species live along the coasts of eastern Africa, southern Asia, Indonesia, and Australasia.

Asia

Africa

Australasia

Breathing

◀ In the middle of the photograph is a small nozzle. This is the siphon. The cone draws in water through the siphon. The water passes over a gill and oxygen is taken out.

FACTS

SIZE

- Larger species of cone shell can grow up to 9 in (23 cm) long.

- They can weigh up to 4 lb 8 oz (2 kg).

- There are more than 600 different species of cone shell.

DID YOU KNOW?

- The cone shell also uses the radula tooth dart in self-defense.

- There are now painkillers on sale based on cone shell toxins.

- It moves by wriggling the bottom of its foot. It traces the scent of a small fish through the water with its siphon.

Feeding

▶ It is a predator that eats marine worms, small fish, mollusks, and even other cone snails. It uses its venomous radula equipped with dart-teeth to capture faster-moving fish. After the prey has been eaten, the cone shell will regurgitate the spines it couldn't digest, as well as the disposable radula tooth.

Sea Slug

The sea slug is a saltwater snail that either does not have a shell or only has a shell inside its body rather than on the outside. It used to have an outer shell but over thousands of years the sea slug has developed without it. This sea creature is almost blind, but it can find other sea slugs by releasing chemicals that they can smell.

Diet

▶ They can be herbivores (only eating plants) or carnivores (only eating meat). They eat algae and sponges.

DID YOU KNOW?

🐚 Some sea slugs can use the chemicals from algae to turn light energy from the sun into chemical energy. These are known as solar-powered sea slugs.

🐚 The sea slugs has a radula—a ribbon of curved teeth. This can be used to scrape or tear food particles.

WHERE DO THEY LIVE?

Sea slugs can be found in various habitats around the world, including coral reefs.

Sea Slug Body

▶ The head does not stand out from the body. Its single foot is a wide, flat muscle. The sea slug moves by tensing and relaxing this muscle and crawling along rocks and other surfaces. The sides of the foot have developed to be fleshy and winglike. The tentacles are situated close to the mouth and are used for finding its way. Behind the tentacles are the organs used for smelling chemicals.

Warning

◀ They have few predators. This is because many are poisonous and they use camouflage or, as seen here, bright colors, to warn off other animals.

FACTS

• They vary in size. Anaspides (sea hares) can be 1 ft 4 in (40 cm).

• Sea slugs live for about a year.

• They are eaten by sea spiders.

SIZE

Dog Whelk

The dog whelk is a meat-eating sea snail. It can only survive out of water for a limited time because it dries out. It prefers to live above a rocky seabed. On the high shore it is threatened by birds and on the lower shore by crabs. It is found in the middle area of the tidal range, neither the high-water nor low-water mark.

WHERE DO THEY LIVE?

They are found around the coasts of Europe and the Atlantic coast of North America.

North America

Europe

Atlantic Ocean

Tidal Pools

▶ Dog whelks can live in tidal pools as long as the pools are not too salty.

Feeding

◀ It prefers to live on rocky shores, where it eats mussels and barnacles. It has a radula tooth to dig holes in the shells of prey and it can produce a shell-softening chemical.

FACTS

SIZE

- Eider ducks will eat a dog whelk shell whole.

- The dog whelk is also known as the Atlantic dogwinkle.

- The shell is usually up to 1.25 in (3 cm) high.

DID YOU KNOW?

- It lives at temperatures of between 3 and 68°F (0–20°C).

- It can be used to produce red-purple and violet dyes.

- Its proboscis can push apart the plates of a barnacle. It can eat a whole barnacle in a day.

Small Shell

▶ Its shell is small and rounded. It has a point like a church spire at the top. The surface has a spiral cord on it. The shell is usually whitish gray, but can also be orange, black, yellow, brown, or a mixture of these colors in bands. Occasionally, the shell is green, blue, or pink. The strength of the waves washing over it determines the shape of the shell.

Cuttlefish

Despite its name, the cuttlefish isn't actually a fish but a mollusk. It floats gently, changing its skin color to camouflage itself as a plant, but then shoots out its tentacles, pulling its prey toward it, biting with its beak. It squirts venom from its mouth, pushing the prey down its throat. If it is attacked, it can shoot out ink, making a cloud to confuse the predator.

WHERE DO THEY LIVE?

They live throughout the oceans of the world, except the Americas.

DID YOU KNOW?

The female cuttlefish lays around 200 small eggs, but dies soon after. Dead female cuttlefish are often washed ashore.

It moves by sucking in water through a funnel and pushing it out like a jet.

It takes just a few seconds for the cuttlefish to change its color.

Eyesight

▶ Cuttlefish cannot see colors. The pupil of the eye—the center—is very distinctive: it is shaped like a letter W.

Sea Chameleon

▶ They are sometimes called the "chameleons of the sea" because they can change their appearance very quickly. They do this to communicate with other cuttlefish and to camouflage themselves. Their blood is a blue-green color. They have three hearts. Two pump blood to the pair of gills, and the third pumps blood around the rest of the body.

Brain

◀ Like squid and octopuses, its behavior is more complex than other mollusks. Behind its eyes it has a large brain shaped like a ring.

FACTS

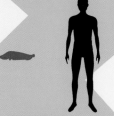

SIZE

● It grows between 12 and 20 in (30–50 cm).

● Its eight arms have suckers along their length. Its two tentacles have suckers at the tips.

● It can weigh up to 26 lb (12 kg).

Mantis Shrimp

These crustaceans spend most of their lives hiding among the rocks in the sea or digging passageways in the seabed. They wait for prey or they hunt, using their powerful claws. Some species have spiny spears to stab prey. Others have a club that quickly smashes prey.

WHERE DO THEY LIVE?

Most species live in tropical or subtropical waters in the Indian and Pacific oceans.

Pacific Ocean

Indian Ocean

Colors

▶ They are many different colors from browns to bright blues, greens, and reds.

Behavior

◀ They can change their color to communicate with other mantis shrimps. Some species hunt during the day, others at night, and others at dawn and dusk.

FACTS

SIZE

- They usually reach 12 in (30 cm) in length.

- There are 400 species of mantis shrimp.

- They can attack animals that are much larger than they are.

DID YOU KNOW?

- They eat snails, crabs, and rock oysters. Those with a spear will attack softer-skinned animals, such as fish.

- Some larger mantis shrimp with a club can break through the glass of an aquarium.

- The peacock mantis shrimp can punch at 50 mph (80 km/h).

Excellent Eyesight

▶ It has possibly the best eyesight in the animal world. The two eyes are on the ends of stalks that can move. The eyes themselves are constantly moving and turn independently of each other—so they can be pointing in different directions at the same time. It is possible they need such good vision because the animals they hunt are almost transparent.

Horseshoe Crab

At rest, this strange sea creature could be mistaken for a shiny stone. And when it moves, it looks like a wind-up toy. We might call it a crab, but it is more closely related to arachnids (spiders) than crustaceans. It is like a spider in heavy armor. Its shell covers its whole body.

Dirty Shell

▶ It has no way of cleaning its shell. When it stops molting, algae and barnacles might become attached to the shell.

WHERE DO THEY LIVE?

It lives off the Atlantic and Gulf coasts of North America, and the coasts of southern and eastern Asia.

North America **Asia**

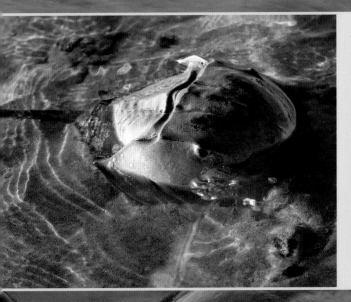

Feeding

◀ It feeds mainly on shellfish, digging them out and crushing them with its strong hind legs. It also eats marine worms, algae, and carrion.

FACTS

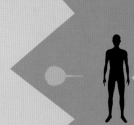

SIZE

- They grow up to 24 in (60 cm) long.
- They can live up to 19 years.
- Although they are saltwater animals, one species was found in freshwater in India.

DID YOU KNOW?

🐚 Young horseshoe crabs can swim upside down in the open ocean.

🐚 It is considered a living fossil. That means that it has changed very little in millions of years.

🐚 Native Americans used its spiked tails as spearheads when they went fishing.

Two-part Body

▶ Its body is split into two parts. The front section is like the spider's head and thorax. The rear section is like the spider's abdomen. Its tail might look like a weapon, but it is mainly used to move itself around or to flip itself back over if it turns upside down. It has five pairs of walking legs, each with pincerlike feet. It has four eyes.

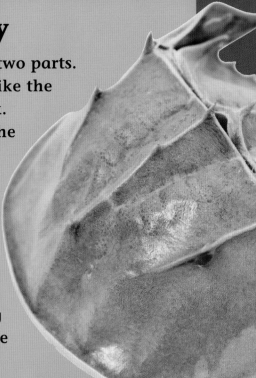

Sea Urchin

The sea urchin is one of the oddest and prettiest animals of the sea, but it is also dangerous. It has glowing colors that make it look like a jewel. However, it can seriously injure any creature unlucky enough to make contact with its spines. The spines stab into flesh and then snap off. They fill the wound with toxins that cause hours of agony.

WHERE DO THEY LIVE?

They live In all the world's seas and oceans, from coastal shallows to the ocean depths.

Spiny Body

▶ The spines are long, up to 12 in (30 cm). There are so many of them that it is difficult to see the body.

Movement

◀ The spines vary in length. They are worked by small muscles, so the urchin can move its spines to fend off attackers or to steer its "walk."

FACTS

SIZE

- Their origins stretch back 450 million years.

- They feed on whatever they can find on the seafloor.

- Colors vary. They can be bright but also dull.

DID YOU KNOW?

Its mouth is on the underside. The teeth scrape algae and other food from the rocks.

Some fish eat sea urchins. They have to attack them from underneath to avoid their dangerous and prickly spines.

The venom of sea urchins does not often kill humans but it can make them unwell.

Sea Hedgehog?

▶ The unusual name of these invertebrates reflects their spiny appearance. "Urchin" is an old English word for a hedgehog. If some of the spines are touched gently, the ones next to it change position and face toward the ones that were touched. Tiny tube feet on the lower side of the body allow the urchin to move around.

Common Starfish

The common starfish is typically a five-armed star-shaped creature. It is most often orange, but can be other colors. It is found when the tide goes out—in the pools of water left behind on rocky shores, underneath boulders, or on sandy beaches.

Tube Feet

▶ Starfish have a row of tubelike feet on the underside that helps to move them along.

WHERE DO THEY LIVE?

Around the coasts of Britain and Ireland, and the north Atlantic from Norway to Senegal.

Norway

North Atlantic

Senegal

Feeding

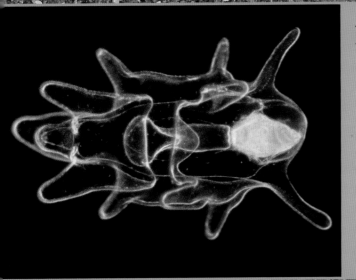

◀ Starfish can push their stomachs out of their mouths so they can digest prey that is too big for them to swallow. They mainly eat mussels, clams, oysters, and sea urchins.

FACTS

SIZE

- A single female starfish can release up to 2.5 million eggs.

- Starfish are often washed up dead onto the shore.

- They can live up to 100 years.

DID YOU KNOW?

🐚 They have five arms that are often turned up slightly at the tip when they are active.

🐚 They can grow to 20 in (52 cm) in diameter, but they are usually 4–12 in (10–30) cm.

🐚 Being shaped like a star, they are radially symmetrical—each arm is exactly the same.

Growing Legs

▶ Sometimes a starfish can be seen with a missing arm. This is not a great loss for a starfish because it can grow the arm back. Sometimes a common starfish is seen with six or more arms. This may be because the starfish accidentally grew two arms to replace one missing one.

Leech

Leeches are flat, wormlike animals that feed on worms, snails, insect larvae, and small aquatic animals. Many freshwater species feed on blood and the bodily fluids of fish. They can be found in shallow waters, hidden among aquatic plants or under stones, logs, and other debris.

Land Leeches

▶ There are leeches that live on land. They lurk in moist habitats such as tropical forests and drop onto animals or people.

DID YOU KNOW?

꩜ Green, brown, or black skin camouflages the leech among vegetation.

꩜ The leech is long and slightly flattened. It swims along with a wavelike motion.

꩜ In the 1800s, using leeches to suck blood was a common medical treatment throughout the United States and Europe.

WHERE DO THEY LIVE?

Throughout the world apart from north of the Arctic Circle.

Bloodsucker

▶ When a leech bites, it holds the sucker in place by making its body stiff. It has semicircular, toothed jaws that are like little saws. It makes a cut in its victim's skin and ejects a mucus that helps the sucker to stick. The simplest way to remove a leech from the skin is with salt: just shake some salt onto the leech's body and it will quickly drop off.

Suckers

◀ Suckers at each end provide a strong grip on stones, plants, or the skin of hosts. At the center of the front sucker are three muscular tooth-lined jaws.

FACTS

SIZE

● There are probably around 700 species of leeches worldwide.

● In winter they burrow in mud.

● They can suck up to 10 times their own body weight in blood.

Sea Cucumber

Sea cucumbers are close cousins of sea urchins and starfish. Many hundreds of species are known. They are cylinder-shaped, a bit like a cucumber or a sausage. They are found in shallow and deep waters throughout the world. They vary widely in color and size.

Feeding

▶ Some sea cucumbers hide in grassy beds. Others burrow in mud and sand. They feed on tiny marine animals and organic matter.

DID YOU KNOW?

If you cut some species of sea cucumber in two, each half grows into a new sea cucumber.

The tiger's tail sea cucumber is by far the largest at 7 ft (2 m) long.

At one end of its body, the sea cucumber has a mouth surrounded by 10–30 food-gathering tentacles.

WHERE DO THEY LIVE?

In all the world's seas and oceans.

Defenses

▶ Sea cucumbers may look harmless, but many of them ooze toxins from their skin. Some Pacific Islanders use the most toxic ones to poison fish by filling reef pools with them. When a sea cucumber is disturbed by an enemy like a crab or a fish, it will fire long, sticky threads from its body to tangle up its enemy.

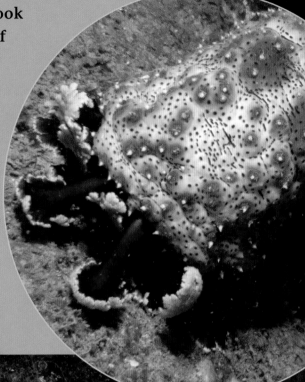

Under Threat

◀ When sea cucumbers are touched and feel threatened, some species suck in water to make themselves big and floppy. Others blow out water to shrink and harden.

FACTS

SIZE

● They can live for up to 5–10 years.

● They range in length from about 1 in to 6 ft (2.5 cm–1.8 m).

● They are eaten as a food in some countries.

Banded Sea Krait

Unlike other marine snakes, the sea krait spends a lot of time on land. It is highly venomous. However, it is not a risk to humans; it hardly ever attacks, not even to try and defend itself. Sea kraits mostly eat conger eels, which they inject with venom and then swallow.

Large Lungs

▶ Inside the sea krait are extra-large lungs. These help it to dive for long periods of time.

WHERE DO THEY LIVE?

Seas and oceans of southeastern Asia, south-western Pacific islands, and north Australia.

Pacific Ocean

Indian Ocean

Other Names

◄ The banded sea krait is known by many other names: snake eel, colubrine sea krait, yellow-lipped sea krait, and banded yellow-lip sea snake.

FACTS

● They rarely attack humans because they are so timid.

● There are around 50 types of sea krait.

● Sea kraits go on land to lay their eggs.

SIZE

DID YOU KNOW?

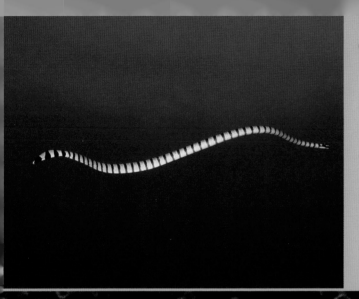

It is happy both in and out of the water. It can spend ten days at a time on land.

The banded sea krait's venom is ten times more toxic than a rattlesnake's venom.

Its small head and tiny fangs mean that it struggles to bite through a wetsuit or skin.

Skin and Scales

► Unlike other sea snakes, the sea krait has long scales running along its stomach. These help it when crawling on land, but are useless for swimming. It also has scales in between its nostrils that push them to the sides of the snout. It sheds its skin every two to six weeks, more often than land snakes.

Leafy Sea Dragon

The leafy sea dragon is a very well camouflaged fish. It can blend into its surroundings very easily because it looks just like seaweed floating around. It belongs to the same family as seahorses. It looks quite like them, with its long snout and bony-plated body.

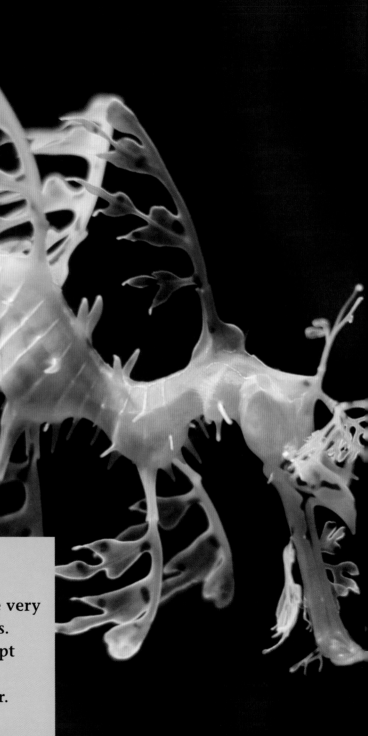

WHERE DO THEY LIVE?

Australia

South Australia's coastline, from Rottnest Island in the west to Kangaroo Island in the east.

Fragile

▶ Sea dragons are very fragile creatures. They are easily swept along and tossed around in the water.

Protected

◀ Divers used to take home leafy sea dragons and keep them as pets. This made the number of them in the wild drop. They are now a protected species.

FACTS

SIZE

- They have no teeth or stomach.

- Like seahorses, males give birth.

- They are slow swimmers and can easily become stranded.

DID YOU KNOW?

Some cultures use sea dragons as an ingredient in traditional medicines.

Newborn and young sea dragons are hunted and eaten by anemones, crabs, and hydroids.

The tail of a male leafy sea dragon will turn bright yellow when he is ready to mate.

Appearance

▶ Leafy sea dragons have long, thin snouts. Their slender trunks are covered in bony rings. They have thin tails that cannot be used for gripping. They have small fins that are not very useful for swimming; they move awkwardly through the water. However, they seem quite happy to tumble and drift in the current of the water, just like seaweed.

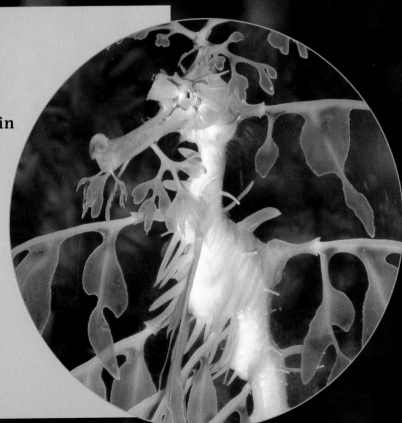

Seahorse

This fish gets its name because it looks like a tiny horse. Although it lives in the sea, it is not a very good swimmer. It moves through the water using a small fin on its back that flutters up to 35 times per second. Even smaller fins near the back of the head are used for steering. The seahorse can die of exhaustion if it is caught up in stormy seas.

WHERE DO THEY LIVE?

In coastal waters in all the warmer oceans and seas of the world.

Catching Food

▶ It lies in wait for small crustaceans and fish to swim by. Having no teeth, the seahorse swallows its prey whole.

Feeding

◀ The seahorse feeds on small fish, brine shrimp, and plankton. Its snout acts like a vacuum cleaner, allowing it to probe weeds and suck up animals into its small mouth.

FACTS

SIZE

● Unlike most other fish, it has a flexible, well-defined neck.

● A male and female seahorse may stay together for life.

● Seahorses swim in an upright position.

DID YOU KNOW?

⚓ The color of seahorses can vary a lot according to each one's habitat.

⚓ There are about 35 different kinds of seahorse. They range in length from less than 0.375 in (1 cm) to about 12 in (30 cm).

⚓ The female lays her eggs inside a pouch along the male's abdomen, where the eggs develop.

Scales and Tails

▶ Instead of scales, the sea horse is covered in plates of tough skin. This gives it some protection against small predators. It has a prehensile tail, which means the tail can grip. It can wrap itself around seaweed to anchor itself or it can wrap around another seahorse. The seahorse is the only fish that can use its tail in this way.

Crown of Thorns Starfish

This spiky killer clamps itself to living corals, then turns its stomach inside-out. It squirts its prey with deadly digestive fluids. It is responsible for killing off large portions of reefs in parts of the Pacific Ocean.

Feeding

▶ The crown of thorns starfish can survive for a long time without food. In the laboratory it has managed without food for nine months.

WHERE DO THEY LIVE?

On coral reefs in the Indian and Pacific oceans. Particularly on the Great Barrier Reef of Australia.

Pacific Ocean

Indian Ocean Australia

Toxic Spines

◀ The crown of thorns starfish has thousands of spines. Each one is up to 2 in (5 cm) long and oozes toxic mucus. They pierce human skin at the slightest touch.

FACTS

SIZE

- It spends about half its time feeding.
- It is the largest starfish in the world.
- Often starfish can survive being cut in half.

DID YOU KNOW?

 One of its few known predators is the giant triton—a huge sea snail.

Unlike other starfish, its arms can grip. Also, other starfish usually have five arms, but the crown of thorns has many more arms.

It can shed an arm to escape a predator and regrow it in six months.

Large Sea Stars

▶ Crown of thorns are large starfish that can reach over 20 in (50 cm) in diameter. Their bodies are covered with sharp spines. They use these as defense against any threat, including humans. Crown of thorns have 13–16 arms that extend out from their body. They vary in color. Their spines are usually a different color than the rest of their body.

Glossary

Algae – sea plants. Some are small, others are large, such as seaweed and kelp.

Antennae – a pair or two pairs of stalks with sensors on the head of a crustacean

Barbel – an organ like a whisker near the mouth of a fish

Camouflage – a method of hiding by disguising with colors and patterns

Carrion – the body of a dead animal that provides food for other animals

Cartilage – a tissue that connects parts of the body. It is less flexible than muscles but not as hard as bone.

Cocoon – a casing made by insect larvae as a protective covering for when they enter the pupa stage

Cretaceous period – the period in history from about 145 million years ago to about 65 million years ago. It was a time when dinosaurs were dominant on the planet.

Crustacean – an arthropod with a toughened outer shell covering its body

Denticle – a small tooth or the placoid scales of a shark, which are like teeth

Electro-sensitive – being sensitive to electric currents. Some fish can recognize the electric fields produced by other fish.

Exoskeleton – a tough body armor. Insects and arachnids have exoskeletons.

Extinction – the death of the last individual of a species

Invertebrate – an animal that does not grow a backbone, such as spiders and insects

Larva – the young stage of animals that change their body structure to become an adult. A caterpillar is the larva stage of a butterfly.

Migration – the traveling over long distances by animals when the seasons change

Mollusk – a group of animals including squid, octopus, and snails. Many have a shell.

Parasite – a smaller animal, such as a flea or a tapeworm, that feeds off a larger one

Plankton – any animals or plant matter that live in seas or freshwater and are unable to swim against the current

Prehensile – a tail that has adapted to grasp and hold objects, such as branches

Proboscis – a long mouthpart used for feeding and sucking

Radula – a ribbon of teeth on mollusks used for cutting food

Regurgitate – to bring back to the mouth undigested, or partly digested, food with which to feed the young

School – a large number of fish or aquatic animals of one kind swimming together

Scute – a bony plate or scale on the shell of a turtle or the skin of crocodilians

Shoal – a large school of fish or other marine animals

Spawning – when eggs are released or deposited by their mother

Spiracle – a small hole behind each eye in all cartilaginous and some bony fish. The hole opens to the mouth and is necessary for breathing.

Streamlined – shaped to have the least resistance to water or air

Submerged – to be under the surface of the water

Thorax – the middle part of the body

Toxins – a poisonous substance made by a living organism

Venom – like a poison, but venom is received through bites and stings

Index

Picture Credits

Alamy: 15t Celebrity, 25t Waterframe, 64/65 Images & Stories; **Big Stock:** 47t Lee Ann Childs, 53b Levent Konuk; **Corbis:** 40/41 Kike Calvo/National Geographic Society; **Dreamstime:** 1, 61b Bluehand, 6, 54/55 Stephan Kerkhofs, 9t Bato461, 11 Maik Schrodter, 11b Ken Kohn, 17b Yobro10, 20/21 Cambliss, 21 both Shawn Jackson, 29b, 37b Subsurface, 35t, 65b Deborah Coles, 37t Mark Doherty, 39t Coldfusion, 41t Roman Zaremba, 41b Ricardo Bazarin, 44/45 Bernd Neeser, 45t Fotografescu, 45b Tim Haynes, 57t Marcin Pawinski, 58/59 Shaun Wilkinson, 59b Rcaucino, 61t Luizrocha, 63t Richard Williamson, 63b Wouter Roesems, 67t Liumangtiger, 69b Asther Lau Choon Siew, 71b Haydn Yip, 75t Fiona Ayerst, 75b Bradford Lumley, 77t Barry Peters, 79t Arenacreative, 79b Doelgautam, 81 Jmaientz, 83b Christopher Moncrieff, 85b Jolanta Dabrowska, 87t Sergey Ponomarev, 87b Michael Ludwig, 89b Daexto, 91b Alison Robertson-Goff, 93t Steffen Foerster, 93b Spfotocz; **FLPA:** 10/11, 30/31 Imagebroker, 12/13, 13t, 50/51, 56/57 Gerard Lacz, 14/15 92/93 Flip Nicklin, 15b Hans Leijinse, 16/17 Luciano Candsani, 22/23 Thomas Marent, 24/25, 28/29 Norbert Wu, 26/27 Paul Hobson, 27b, 85t David Hosking, 32/33 Richard Herrmann, 34/35 Brigitte Wilms, 36/37 Norbert Probst, 38/39, 39b Matthias Breiter, 42/43 Mark Smith/Photo Researchers, 43 both, 66/67 Malcolm Schuyl, 46/47 Frank Lane, 47t Richard Nowitz/Photo Researchers, 48/49 J Van Arkel/Photo Researchers, 49t Tom McHugh/ Photo Researchers, 52/53, 53t, 62/63, 88/89 Fred Bavendam, 60/61 Reinhard Dirscherl, 68/69 Silvestris, 70/71 J W Alker, 72/73, 73t Steve Trewhella, 74/75, 76/77 Birgitte Wilms, 78/79 Piotr Naskrecki, 80/81, 83 D P Wilson, 82/83 Bert Pijs, 84/85 Michael Rose, 90/91 Judith Thomandl, 94/95 Helmut Corneli; **Fotolia:** 9b Jose Hernaiz; **Getty:** 8/9 Franco Banfi/Waterframe, 25b Ronald Modray Sports Imagery; **iStock:** 49b Amanda Rohde, 59t Stephanie Phillips; **NOAA:** 3, 65t, 69t, 81t; **Photos.com:** 17t, 19t; **Photoshot:** 51b Gerard Lacz; **Klaus Rudloff:** 51t; **Science Photo Library:** 13b Peter Scoones; **Shutterstock:** 18/19 Bernd Neeser, 19b Melvin Lee, 23t Andrew L, 23b Anthony Hall, 29t Rich Carey, 31t Driovier, 31b Pinosub, 33t Cynoclub, 33b Dirk-Jan Mattaar, 35b Judex, 55t Mark Doherty, 55b Aqua4, 57b Kletr, 67b Eric Isselle, 71t Ligio, 73b Martin Fowler, 77b Teguh Tirtaputra, 89t Dan Exton, 91t James Blinn, 95t Olga Khorushunova, 95b Kasia; **US Fish & Wildlife Services:** 27t